Underground Towns, Treetops, and Other Animal Hiding Places

Underground
Towns,
Treetops,
and Other
Animal
Hiding
Places

By Monica Halpern

NATIONAL GEOGRAPHIC

WASHINGTON, D.C.

Founded in 1888, the National Geographic Society is one of the largest nonprofit scientific and educational organizations in the world. It reaches more than 285 million people worldwide each month through its official journal, NATIONAL GEOGRAPHIC, and its four other magazines; the National Geographic Channel; television documentaries; radio programs; films; books; videos and DVDs; maps; and interactive media. National Geographic has funded more than 8,000 scientific research projects and supports an education program combating geographic illiteracy.

For more information, please call
1-800-NGS-LINE (647-5463) or write to the following address:

National Geographic Society
1145 17th Street N.W.
Washington, D.C. 20036-4688
U.S.A.

Visit us online at www.nationalgeographic.com/books

For information about special discounts for bulk purchases, please contact
National Geographic Books Special Sales at ngspecsales@ngs.org

For rights or permissions inquiries, please contact National Geographic
Books Subisidiary Rights: ngbookrights@ngs.org

Published by National Geographic Society.
Washington, D.C. 20036

Design by Project Design Company
Photo Editor: Annette Kiesow
Project Editor: Anita Schwartz

Printed in the United States

**Library of Congress
Cataloging-in-Publication Data**

Halpern, Monica.
   Underground towns, treetops, and other animal hiding places / by Monica Halpern.
      p. cm. -- (National Geographic science chapters)
   ISBN 978-1-4263-0183-4 (library)
   1. Habitat (Ecology)--Juvenile literature.   2. Animal defenses--Juvenile literature.   I. Title.
   QH541.14.H33 2007
   591.47--dc22

                    2007007894

Photo Credits
Cover: © Staffan Widstrand/CORBIS; Spine, Endpaper, 22: © Michael & Patricia Fogden/CORBIS; 2-3: © Robert C. Nunnington/Getty Images; 6, 8, 9: © Robert Yin/CORBIS; 10: © Tony Evans/Timelaps/Getty Images; 12: © Ralph A. Clevenger/CORBIS; 13 (top): © Fiona Sunquist; 13 (inset): © Hope Ryden/ National Geographic Image Collection; 14: © Robert Hynes/ National Geographic Image Collection;
15: © Will & Deni McIntyre/CORBIS; 16: © Charles C. Place/The Image Bank/Getty Images; 17, 18: © Jupiterimages; 19: © Jason Edwards/Bio-Images; 20: © Anthony Bannister/Gallo Images/CORBIS; 22 (inset): © Wayne Lawler/Auscape; 23: © Stephen Frink/CORBIS; 24: © Thorsten Milse/Getty Images; 25, 32: © Shutterstock; 26, 27: © Raymond Gehman/CORBIS; 28: © Alan Root/Auscape; 29: © Joe McDonald/CORBIS; 30: © Martin Harvey/Gallo Images/CORBIS; 33: © Beverly Joubert/NGS/Getty Images;
34: © W. Perry Conway/CORBIS; 35: © Raymond K. Gehman/National Geographic Image Collection.

Endsheets: Carmine bee-eater birds gather at the nests they carved in a cliff wall.

Contents

A dingo hides with her newborn pups in a cave.

Why Animals Hide

Staying alive is a constant struggle for most animals. Every day they must find food. They must take care of their young. They must stay away from predators. They also have to protect themselves from extreme weather.

Animals have found many different ways to protect themselves. Some animals can run very fast. When an enemy approaches, they run away. Many animals keep themselves safe by hiding. They sleep, eat, and protect their young in a hiding place.

Animals hide everywhere—in backyards, forests, deserts, and oceans. Wherever there are animals, there are hiding places. You can find clues to where animals are hiding. Look for holes in the ground or hollows in trees. These are the doorways to animal hiding places.

Some animals dig their secret hideaways underground. Others build hiding places high off the ground. Some move into hiding places that other animals have left.

An Australian wombat hides in a hole it has dug in the ground.

An eel hides among the coral in ocean waters.

Some animals live alone. Others share their hiding places. Some animals live in groups in large homes with many rooms.

Some animals use their hiding places all year long. Other animals use hiding places only during certain seasons.

Let's take a look at some secret hideaways animals call home.

Almost blind, the mole uses its strong sense of smell to find food.

Chapter 1

Hiding Underground

The mole is one animal that seems made for building an underground hideaway. Its front legs make it an excellent digger. They grow outward from the mole's shoulders and end in paddle-shaped paws. The mole digs with a swimming motion. It shovels first with one paw and then the other. It can dig through several feet (a meter) of soft earth in a minute.

Aboveground, the mole is slow and clumsy. But it seldom needs to leave its hiding place. It spends most of its time traveling through its tunnels looking for food.

A ghost crab crawls out of its hideaway in the sand.

Other animals dig underground hiding places at the beach. The ghost crab digs a tunnel in the sand. The crab stays in its cool hideaway during the heat of the day. It plugs the opening with damp sand to keep its enemies out. At night, the ghost crab comes out of its tunnel to find food.

Sometimes, animals share their hiding places. If you came upon a gopher tortoise in its burrow, or underground home, you would probably find a surprise. The gopher tortoise often has a roommate—a snake!

The gopher tortoise shares its burrow with a rattlesnake.

The gopher tortoise builds a hiding place by digging a hole in the sand. Once the hole is finished, a rattlesnake moves in. The two animals spend each day together, peacefully enjoying their cool hiding place. At night, when the outside temperature drops, they come out to find food.

The rooms and tunnels of a prairie dog town are important hideaways for many prairie animals.

Still other animals hide underground in groups. Prairie dogs live in big underground towns. A prairie dog town has narrow tunnels leading to many different rooms.

There are rooms for sleeping, storing food, and raising pups. There are even rooms that are used as bathrooms. The underground rooms are warmer in the winter and cooler in the summer than the prairie above them.

A Gila woodpecker carves out a
nest hole in a saguaro cactus in
the Sonora Desert in Arizona.

Chapter 2

Hiding Up High

Not all animals live in hiding places underground. Some live in holes high up in trees or even in tall cactuses.

In the desert, Gila woodpeckers make their nests in giant cactuses called saguaros. They drill into the saguaro with their sharp beaks. Sap from the cactus oozes out to form a hard lining for the nest. These nests make comfortable homes. They protect the birds from hot desert days and cold desert nights.

An Indian scops owl nests in a tree at night.

Young raccoons hide in a hollow log on the ground.

Some animals move into treetop homes that were built by other animals. Empty woodpecker holes make good hiding places for other birds, bats, and even mice. Some of these animals bring in leaves, grasses, bark, or feathers to make comfortable beds. Many raccoons make their dens in tree holes, usually above the ground.

Weaver birds are well hidden in their treetop hideaway.

In southern Africa, weaver birds share one big treetop hideaway. As many as 125 pairs of weaver birds may live together in one big straw nest. These nests can stretch 15 feet (4.5 meters) across. The group nest has one roof, but many rooms. Each room has its own entrance.

Weaver birds use the same nest year after year. New birds join the group by adding on their own room. If the nest gets too large and heavy, it can fall to the ground. Then, the birds move to another tree and start building a new home.

A trap-door spider hides inside a tunnel waiting to grab an insect passing by.

Chapter 3

Hiding to Catch Food

Some animals use their hiding places for more than protection. Like other animals, the trap-door spider uses its underground hiding place to stay safe. But the trap-door spider also uses its hiding place to get food.

The spider builds a tunnel by scraping the ground with its bristly jaws. It lines the tunnel with silk that it spins from its body. Then it makes a door of silk and dirt.

The spider hides behind its door. When it senses any movement outside the door, it pops out. If an insect is there, the spider grabs it and eats it.

The ant lion is another animal—actually an insect—that uses its hiding place to catch food. It digs a sandy pit and buries itself. Only its jaws stick out. Then, it waits. When an ant or other crawling insect comes too close, it falls into the pit. The ant lion pops out of the sand, grabs the fallen prey, and eats it.

Buried at the bottom of these circular sand pits, an ant lion (shown in the smaller picture) waits for its prey to fall in.

A goby fish and a blind shrimp (right) live together on the sea floor.

Creatures in ocean hideaways sometimes help each other catch food. The snapping shrimp digs a hiding place. Once the burrow is dug out, a goby fish moves in and helps the shrimp. The shrimp is blind. It rests an antenna on the Goby's tail. When an enemy comes along, the goby flicks its tail to warn the shrimp. Then, the two hurry back to their burrow to hide.

Polar bear mothers build dens, often in snowbanks, where they spend the winter with their cubs. Around March, they start coming out of their dens to search for food.

Chapter 4

Hiding to Survive the Weather

Many animals live in the same place all year long. Other animals find hiding places to survive the seasons. They hide to protect themselves during very hot or cold weather.

A watchful meerkat stands in front of his home. The sleeping chamber of a meerkat burrow is 6-8 feet underground. This keeps them warmer in winter and cooler in summer.

Surviving Cold Weather

Garter snakes spend the spring and summer in marshes in Canada. In September, thousands of the snakes travel as far as 10 miles (16 kilometers) to reach deep pits where they spend the cold winter months. In spring, about three weeks after the last snow melts, the snakes slither back to their warm-weather homes.

Garter snakes slither out of their winter homes in spring.

An American black bear cub peers out of its winter hideaway.

Bears also find a special place to spend
the winter. When the weather turns cold in
late fall, a bear looks for shelter in a cave.
It makes a warm bed with twigs and grass.
Then it curls up and goes into a deep sleep
called hibernation. During this time, female
bears give birth to their cubs. In early spring,
something tells the bear that it is time to
wake up, and it leaves its winter hiding place.

Surviving the Heat

Extreme heat can be just as dangerous as extreme cold. Animals that live where it is very hot need hideaways for protection, too.

The African lungfish lives in a very hot, dry area. For most of the year, it swims in rivers or lakes. Like other fish, it breathes through its gills.

But when its watery home dries up during a time of no rain, the lungfish buries itself in the riverbed or lake bottom. It can sleep there for several years without food or water. It breathes air. It is protected from dryness by a covering of slime and old skin.

An African lungfish can live for years buried in the mud.

A banner-tailed kangaroo rat hops like a tiny kangaroo.

The banner-tailed kangaroo rat lives in the southwestern United States and northern Mexico. It survives desert life by staying underground during the day. At night, temperatures drop and the kangaroo rat leaves its burrow to find food. As it eats, it also absorbs the moisture formed on desert plants in the nighttime air. The kangaroo rat actually drinks little or no water.

A mother warthog dozes at the entrance to her burrow with her piglets.

Chapter 5

Hiding to Protect the Young

Many animals use hiding places when they are raising their young. Baby animals often can't protect themselves.

Warthogs

Female warthogs raise their young in underground hiding places. These animals live on the African grasslands. Before she has her babies, the warthog moves into an empty burrow. Here, the warthog babies will be protected from the hot African days and chilly nights. No enemies can reach them.

Once the warthog babies are a little older, the family moves outside to graze. If an enemy comes along, the mother warthog hustles her babies into their burrow. She backs in after them, pointing her sharp tusks outward at the enemy.

Bee-eaters

Birds called bee-eaters live on cliffs in Africa. They eat bees and wasps. These birds live in family groups called clans. Several clans live together in a colony.

A parent carmine bee-eater feeds its chick (right).

Carmine bee-eater birds carve rows of nest holes in a cliff.

Bee-eaters are tunnel makers. Before they lay their eggs, the parents-to-be chip away at the cliff wall with their bills. Once a tunnel is started, the birds make it bigger by kicking out the dirt with their feet. Tunnels can be as long as 6 feet (2 meters).

Other clan members help dig the tunnels. They also take turns sitting on the eggs and feeding the chicks. With the whole community helping out, the chicks have a better chance of growing up.

Gray wolf pups peer out from their den.

Wolves

Early in spring, the members of a wolf pack take turns digging a deep den in a hillside. There, the female leader has five to seven pups. Curled up around the tiny pups, the mother keeps them warm. At first, the pups live off their mother's milk.

As the pups grow, all the members of the pack help take care of them. The adult wolves bring the pups food, play with them, and protect them from any enemies. Soon, the pups are big enough to learn to hunt. The pack doesn't need the den any longer.

A young boy looks to see what animal may have built this underground hideaway.

Next time you are taking a walk, look closely. Look for clues that animals may be hiding. See if you can find some animal hiding places. If you find an animal's hiding place, don't disturb it. Watch from a distance. Be patient and you might see who lives there!

How to Write an A+ Report

1. Choose a topic.

- Find something that interests you.
- Make sure it is not too big or too small.

2. Find sources.

- Ask your librarian for help.
- Use many different sources: books, magazine articles, and Web sites.

3. Gather information.

- Take notes. Write down the big ideas and interesting details.
- Use your own words.

4. Organize information.

- Sort your notes into groups that make sense.

- Make an outline. Put your groups of notes in the order you want to write your report.

5. Write your report.

- Write an introduction that tells what the report is about.

- Use your outline and notes as you write to make sure you say everything you want to say in the order you want to say it.

- Write an ending that tells about your report.

- Write a title.

6. Revise and edit your report.

- Read your report to make sure it makes sense.

- Read it again to check spelling, punctuation, and grammar.

7. Hand in your report!

Glossary

burrow	a hole an animal makes underground to use as shelter
clan	a group of families related in some way
colony	a group of clans
den	a place where a wolf, bear, or other wild animal lives
hibernation	a deep sleep some animals go into to survive winter
hollow	an empty space inside a tree
marsh	low-lying wetland where grassy plants grow
prairie	a large area of flat or hilly land, usually covered with tall or short grasses, but no trees
predator	an animal that hunts and eats other animals
saguaro	a giant cactus that grows in the desert of the southwestern United States and Mexico
tunnel	a long underground passage

Further Reading

• Books •

National Geographic. *My First Pocket Guide: Backyard Wilderness*. Washington, D.C.: National Geographic Society, 2003. Grades 1–5, 80 pages.

National Geographic. *My First Pocket Guide: Reptiles & Amphibians*. Washington, D.C.: National Geographic Society, 2001. Grades 1–5, 80 pages.

Perry, Phyllis J. *Animals Under the Ground*. London: Franklin Watts, 2002. Grades 3–6, 64 pages.

Squire, Ann O. *Animal Homes* (True Books: Animals). New York: Children's Press, 2002. Grades 3–6, 48 pages.

Wilkes, Angela. *Animal Homes* (Kingfisher Young Knowledge). Kingfisher, 2003. Grades 1–3, 48 pages.

• Web Sites •

Enchanted Learning
http://www.enchantedlearning.com/Home.htm

National Geographic Kids Magazine
www.nationalgeographic.com/kids/creature_feature

National Park Service
http://www.nps.gov/wica/Prairie_Dog.htm

ThinkQuest
http://library.thinkquest.org/TQ0312800/hibernate.htm

Wisconsin Department of Natural Resources Environmental Education for Kids
http://dnr.wi.gov/eek

Index